Social Media
and
Digital Scholarship
for
Academic Research
A User's Guide

By

Dan Remenyi and Sue Greener

Social Media and Digital Scholarship for Academic Research - A User's Guide

First edition, November 2016

ISBN: 978-1-911218-21-0

Published by: ACPIL, Reading, RG4 9SJ, United Kingdom, info@academic-conferences.org Printed by Lightning Source UK Ltd. Available from www.academic-bookshop.com

This book should be used in conjunction with the following Facebook Group

https://www.facebook.com/groups/680234778819832/

This is a repository of all the URLs referred to in this book and access to it is available on request. See Appendix 3 for details of the Group.

Many product names have been referred to in this book. The authors and publisher state that these are the trademarks and copyrights of the firm whose property they are.

Contents

Preface iii

About the use of this book vi

Prologue viii

About the Authors x

Other books in the series xi

1. Academe, the Internet and the Web 1

2. The Internet and the Web 3

3. Web 1.0, Web 2.0, Web 3.0 and Web 4.0 5

4. Non-Internet and Non-Web ICT developments 9

5. Social media and digital scholarship - some critical
    definitions 13

6. Strengths, Weaknesses, Opportunities and Threats (SWOT) ... 17

7. Some most important applications for Digital Scholarship 25

8. Intellectual property rights 35

9. Incorporating social media and digital scholarship into a
    research design 39

10. Fast tracking the literature review by identifying the most
    important papers 43

11. Research question development 47

12. Identifying and working with knowledgeable informants 51

13. Data capture using social media 57

14. Tools for quantitative and qualitative data analysis 61

15. The implications of social media on research ethics protocols 63

16. Support for research processes 67

17. Dissemination of research findings and establishing an academic reputation 69

18. The Cloud 73

19. Utilities 77

20. Will the Web and the Internet change the essential nature of scholarship? 85

21. Current Action and the Future of Digital Scholarship 87

Reference list 91

Appendix 1:   A Note for Establishing a Facebook Group 92

Appendix 2:   A Note on using Twitter to explore research connections 93

Appendix 3:   A Note on the Facebook Group associated with the Seminar 94

Appendix 4:   A note on how to start a research blog and profile on Wordpress 95

Appendix 5:   A Note on Edublog 96

Appendix 6:   A Note on Researchgate 97

Appendix 7:   A Note on Eduroam 98

An account of the development of ICT in the academic process through the experiences of one scholar 99

Index 107

Preface

The scope of this book is a little less than it would be if it addressed Life, Liberty, Happiness and Everything Else in the Universe. And as the book developed it became clear that its scope was truly enormous. Therefore it is important to state some delimiters around how this subject has been treated.

 One of the assumptions we have made is that readers of this book will have had some exposure to the concept of academic research and will know in broad terms what is required to complete a research dissertation or to have a paper published in a peer reviewed academic journal, and we will therefore not address in any detail the standards that are required for this type of work. We will however discuss at a relatively high level, the processes which are required in order to ensure the high quality of scholarship demanded by rigorous academic research.

Over the years ICT has insinuated itself into many different facets of academic teaching and we will make relatively minor reference to many of these. The emphasis of the book focuses on the research aspects of academe and how digital scholarship, as seen through applications available on the Internet and the Web, has impacted the way that research is conducted. There are probably two major aspects to this.

Firstly, scholarship has been facilitated by the wide range of applications which can now be accessed through a number of different communication and computing devices ranging from smart phones to tablets and larger computers. These types of applications can make the tasks of the researcher easier and more convenient than ever before, at least for those who have mastered this technology. Careful use of the technology has lead to better research being conducted in shorter periods of time. Sometimes the use of this technology has been referred to as e-Research, a term which on its own is not especially useful. In this book the Internet and Web applications which may be used to facilitate academic research are simply understood as a tool set which a scholar may use.

But there is a second impact of the Internet and the Web on scholarship, which does not relate to any particular applications, but rather to a shift in attitude towards a more open view of academic research. Some 20 years ago when a research student  began a research degree, he or she was expected to establish the research question and design an approach to finding a suitable answer to it in discussion with his or her supervisor and by reference to the university or business school's library facilities. Where empirical research was involved a student might make some limited contacts with knowledgeable informants outside. When data was required the research student often struggled to make any contacts and get access to appropriate people. The general approach to the research was inward looking, relying on internal university resources.

Largely because of the Internet and the Web academic research has become much more open involving networks of academics, other researchers and knowledgeable informants. The research student is now encouraged to look outside the close relationship between the student and supervisor to find new ideas and new information concerning the research question and how it might be answered. The research process is now a much more open affair than it ever was before and this makes academic research more interesting and provides a greater opportunity for success. The reason for this is that by sharing information and opinions researchers can both have their ideas tested by other as well as have the opportunity to discover and reflect on the thoughts of others. In the dialogue which ensues there will inevitably be a degree of critique, which is essential to academic success. This is a win-win situation which incorporates the essence of the dialectic which in its modern application is sometimes referred to as the Law of Reciprocity i.e. I will tell you what I think about your research if you will tell me what you think about mine.

There was at one time concern that this type of openness might lead to confusion and to a lowering of academic standards. This has not happened. In fact it may lead to an improvement of academic standards.

Academic research now requires a demonstration that something of value has been added to the body of theoretical knowledge and that this new knowledge can be applied in a useful way within the community.

In short the current view of academic research which has resulted from this openness has in no way led to any reduction in the high standards required for quality academic performance.

Dan Remenyi
dan.remenyi@gmail.com

About the use of this book

This book brings together two subjects which are closely interconnected, but which some readers will see as being quite separate. The first of these is social media, which refers to a number of applications, the object of which, in the context of this book, is to connect academic researchers as well as potential knowledgeable informants who could assist with providing information and data for the research. When understood this way social media is only a part of the much broader subject of digital scholarship.

Most importantly this book is essentially a user's guide which means that it provides information as to how to access particular types of functionality using the facilities provided by the Internet and the Web. It cannot do this successfully without ensuring that a reader has a considerable amount of background and contextual information which will allow him or her to make sense of the applications available. For that reason the book offers information about the academic research context and the issues that relate to how the Internet and the Web affect the academic research process.

However, it should be noted that this is not a book on how to conduct academic research, which is quite a different subject, and readers need to be reasonable familiar with before embarking on this book.

There are few if any other environments which are as large and as complex and are subject to as much continuous change as the Internet and the Web. Furthermore, there is actually no way of knowing how much information or data there is on the Web. It is also impossible to fully map the unknown and ever increasing number of applications which are available to support any particular activity or profession. It is therefore only possible to give what has to be a relatively narrow but well focused view of how academic research has been impacted by this technology.

Whenever anyone writes about the phenomenon of the Internet and the Web their thoughts are almost out-of-date before the ink is dry on the paper. This is a quintessential dimension of the nature of the biggest collection of human activity ever initiated. Therefore this book is being written in the knowledge that it can never be a complete account of what is available to academic researchers and also that the material which the book contains will need continual updating.

Learning about the Internet and the Web and what it can do is perhaps the modern day equivalent of the Myth of Sisyphus, but it may also be seen as the ultimate adventure into an interesting if not exciting world where there are many unknowns, but also many great advantages to those who master the subject.

This book should be used in conjunction with the following Facebook Group

https://www.facebook.com/groups/680234778819832/

This is a repository of all the URLs referred to in this book and access to it is available on request. See Appendix 3 for details of the Group.

Prologue

The title of this book begs the Question, How do Social Media and Digital Scholarship relate to one another?

From an academic point of view digital scholarship relates to all the applications available through the Internet and the Web which may be used to facilitate the teaching and learning endeavour. This of course includes research activities. There are literally hundreds of these if not a thousand. Social media on the other hand, refers to the Internet and the Web applications that allow scholars and students to reach out to others who might wish to share ideas or even collaborate in furthering their studies or their research. There are dozens of these. Each university or research institute will have its own preferred software applications and individual researchers need to be familiar with what support the university offers for which applications.

The diagram below shows how these applications may be understood as separate sets within these two groups.

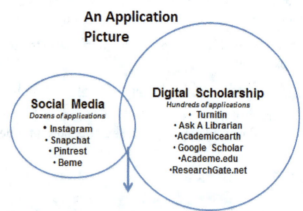

An Application Picture

Social Media
Dozens of applications
- Instagram
- Snapchat
- Pintrest
- Beme

Digital Scholarship
Hundreds of applications
- Turnitin
- Ask A Librarian
- Academicearth
- Google Scholar
- Academe.edu
- ResearchGate.net

Primary Applications: Facebook, Twitter, LinkedIn, Google+
Secondary Applications: Youtube

There is a substantial amount of overlap between social media and digital scholarship when social media applications are used to facilitate research. The principal applications where this overlap is apparent is in Facebook, Twitter, Linkedin and Google +. There is also much overlap in the way YouTube is frequently used. This overlap is an important issue in understanding this subject.

About the authors

Dr Dan Remenyi specialised in research methodology and new technology. He was for more than a decade a Visiting Professor in Information Systems Management at the School of Systems and Data Studies at Trinity College, University of Dublin. He teaches Research Methodology and Sociology of Research as well as supervising academic researchers and works extensively with research candidates and their supervisors at both doctoral and masters level. He has examined both masters and doctoral degrees in a number of universities in several countries. He has authored or co-authored more than 30 books and some 50 academically refereed papers. He is published in all 4 of the 'A' rated Journals in the United Kingdom in Information Systems Management. Some of his books have been translated into Chinese, Japanese and Romanian. He holds a B Soc Sc, an MBA and a PhD.

Dr Sue Greener is Principal Lecturer at the University of Brighton Business School teaching Learning & Development, HRM, Business Context and Research Methods and has received a Teaching Excellence award from the University. She researches, advises and supervises in the fields of e-learning strategy, technology enhanced learning and reflective learning. She teaches and examines at both master's and doctoral level. She is Editor of the academic journal Interactive Learning Environments, published by Routledge. She holds a BA, an MBA and an Ed D. Sue is also a member of FHEA and a Chartered FCIPD.

Other books in this series

- Field Methods for Academic Research,
- Case Study Research,
- Grounded Theory,
- Statistics using Excel,
- Ethics Protocols and Ethics Committees,
- Writing Up Your Dissertation
- Research Dictionary
- Leading Issues in Research Methods

Social Media and Digital Scholarship for Academic Research

1. Academe, the Internet and the Web

Before addressing the detail of the subject of Social Media and Digital Scholarship for Academic Research it is worth pointing out that development in ICT have had a dramatic impact on the lives of the individuals who have had access to this technology. ICT has insinuated itself into almost every aspect of the lives 2 billion or so people who have regular access to it. Inter alia it has changed the way that people relate to one another, the way that they transact their business, the way that they learn and the way in which they are entertained. What is important to point out is that these developments in the technology, which most people experience directly or indirectly through the Web and the Internet is part of an ongoing evolutionary process which is likely to continue and will no doubt result in there being new ways by which individuals will conduct the business of their lives. The rate at which these evolutionary developments are delivered is unknowable and therefore changes to the way that academic research is impacted by further developments in ICT in the future will render the applications described here a matter of historical record.

Academic endeavours have always required individuals to be well informed about what is already known in their subject area and what the current thinking is about their topic. It is on top of what is already known that academic research delivers new contributions to the body of knowledge. It is by adding new or original insights that the body of knowledge develops. There are two reasons why it is especially beneficial for the academic researcher to closely monitor current thinking in his or her topic. Firstly, the discussion in the research community suggests what are the more interesting aspects of the topic that are valuable to explore and secondly by knowing what is being discussed the academic researcher can avoid undertaking projects which might in some way duplicate what is currently work-in-progress elsewhere.

In the pre-Internet era being "well informed about what is already known in the subject area" often meant much visiting of libraries and other sources of information, while closely monitoring current thinking in a topic often required a significant amount of slow postal correspondence or indeed travel to other universities and/or institutes. One of the effects of the Internet and the Web is that different resources and individuals around the world can be accessed in a much more efficient and effective way. The Internet and the Web may be understood as a funnel through which a significant part of the resources required for academic research can be accessed. In addition to this the Internet and the Web makes available to the academic researchers many of the tools which he or she might need to pursue a research project.

Using this technique, it is now possible, at least theoretically, for a research degree to be initiated, managed and completed by a researcher without having to leave his or her desk.

It is this shift in how academic research can be performed that is the essence of Digital Scholarship and one of the more significant catalysts or agents in this new approach is referred to as Social Media. This is an evolving subject, and new concepts and approaches to the use of this technology are being developed on an almost daily basis, which leads one to recall the comment made by the Red Queen (the Red Queen Hypothesis) in Alice in Wonderland[1].

---

[1] The Red Queen Hypothesis states that you have to keep running to stay relatively in the same position.

2. The Internet and the Web

The terms Internet and Web are sometimes used interchangeably, but in fact they refer to 2 different aspects of the facilities that are commonly used to engage in Digital scholarship.

The Internet refers to the hardware and software and communications technology, which allows different computers around the world to communicate with each other. The Internet was developed primarily for the purposes of communication of which e-mail is the most commonly used feature and an essential social media.

On the other hand, the term Web refers to the multitude of data repositories which have been created by individuals, corporate entities, NGOs and governments around the world, and which can be accessed through the communication tools which are made available through the Internet.

However, as mentioned above, these words are often used interchangeably to mean a combination of both the above two facilities.

3. Web 1.0, Web 2.0, Web 3.0 and Web 4.0

Different terms or names have been used to describe the development of the Web and differentiate between the different levels of functionality which have become available to users as the Web has evolved since the 1990s.

It is common to use the terms Web 1.0, Web 2.0 and Web 3.0 to indicate different levels of sophistication, which have been used by web developers when creating facilities on the Web. The use of this terminology is reminiscent of how computers were described in the mid-20th century as being either first-generation or second-generation, and then third generation. However, there were so many innovations within computer technology that the community decided to drop this generation counting approach to describing different levels of technological sophistication. It is very likely that this will also happen in the case of websites, although there are currently some individuals who wish to talk about Web 4.0 as being the latest development.

Web 1.0 is a term used in retrospect to describe the early days of the web where the primary function was to make available information. Thus the emphasis of this level of technology was often described as *"brochureware"* i.e. Web pages substituted for written information previously made available on paper. There was little else available than one way communication. Nonetheless this had considerable value to many academics.

Web 2.0 shifted the emphasis to two-way communication. Chat pages were available as well as discussions by e-mail. Users of the Web were encouraged to respond or make comments and Web suppliers could engage in discussion. Websites began to remember some of the details of previous visits. Web 2.0 delivered the possibility of collaboration across the Web and was thus the foundation on which social media could be built.

Web 3.0 refers to the increasingly sophisticated applications of technology to Websites that have been introduced over the past

5

decade. Applications developed for Web 3.0 are more user friendly and use graphics better. They are more intuitive. More cookies are used. Some websites also started to employ a higher degree of artificial intelligence. Machine learning and machine reasoning are the key issues here.

Web 4.0 is a term used to describe so-called ultra-intelligent electronic agents. It is not entirely clear what this might actually mean to users. It is possible that at the present time this term is largely hyperbole. If it does have a major impact on how the Web will be used it is likely to be some time away.

Web changes are continuous. New ideas on how to make websites more attractive appear regularly and the popularity of old favourites fade. Keeping fully up-to-date is virtually impossible. But it is critical to have a solid working knowledge of what the Internet and the Web can do for the academic scholar. This knowledge may be referred to as digital literacy. It is quite important for academic researchers to be relatively up-to-date so as not to be left behind.

Links for further information:

A brief overview, definition and timeline of the progression of the Web

https://lifeboat.com/ex/Web.3.0

Web 4.0: The Ultra-Intelligent Electronic Agent is Coming:

http://tinyurl.com/zt4vqvg

There is some particularly interesting video on this subject

https://www.youtube.com/watch?v=bCeV--mnAuQ

http://tinyurl.com/qxw452h

4. Non-Internet and Non-Web ICT developments

First of all it is well to remember that academics have always been enthusiastic about developments in ICT that can assist the process of scholarship. Universities were early adopters of large mainframe computers in the 1960s. Admittedly they had a relatively limited range of applications which only involved statistical and mathematical work and some text processing. When word processing became viable in the 1970s universities were again in the forefront of its use. At this point were processors were centralised on specialised or dedicated machines and did not become accessible as a software product to the majority of academic researchers until the early 1980s. With built-in spelling and grammar checkers this technology had a significant impact on academic output.

Over the years universities have been big spenders on ICT but much of this has been for scientific and engineering type applications. The range of quantitative data analytical products has been extensively expanded and these applications became important to social scientists. SPSS has for many years been a most important product as has its rival SAS.

There was in universities an increasing use of personal computer products. Microsoft Office was extensively taught to undergraduates. Word and PowerPoint became tools for everyone and Excel has offered routine statistical analysis to those dealing with numbers.

Digital scholarship may be seen as the next step in the application of ICT technology to the development of the university's exploration of how to improve its efficiency and effectiveness.

Links for further information:

Top Statistical Analysis Software Products:

http://www.capterra.com/statistical-analysis-software/

http://tinyurl.com/zd5zy6u

http://r4stats.com/articles/popularity/

https://en.wikipedia.org/wiki/List_of_statistical_packages

http://www.predictiveanalyticstoday.com/top-statistical-software/

In addition to the usual data analytic software there are now a number of data mining products available and there is a growing emphasis on Data Mining and Big Data.

Data Mining

https://en.wikipedia.org/wiki/Educational_data_mining

http://tinyurl.com/h2fn38n

Big data - What is it and why it matters:

http://www.sas.com/en_us/insights/big-data/what-is-big-data.html

What's Up With Big Data Ethics?

http://tinyurl.com/ztqx5fu

Various data analytical sales organizations provide white papers on this subject which attempt to explain the options available.

Qualitative data analysis

Tools which assist with qualitative data analysis come under the heading of CAQDAS or Computer Assisted Qualitative Data AnalysiS.

With regards to qualitative data analysis there are several important software packages and NVIVO and ATLAS.ti are the most frequently used. These products are not trivial to use and they require time to learn and to upload the parameters to be used on the data. But when fully installed they do provide considerable analytical power.

There are numerous other applications which facilitate scholarship including workflow software, project management products and diary systems to mention only three areas of interest.

Links for further information:

https://workflowy.com/

https://www.youtube.com/watch?v=hwqu_ZIRN0M

 There are products which assist the production of written work such as voice recognition software, an area which has improved substantially over recent years and has made creating documents much quicker. The market leader is Dragon®, which now requires very little in the way of voice training, but which of course can have its accuracy improved by giving enough attention to the training issues involved.

Voice Recognition Software – Reviews and Comparisons:

http://www.toptenreviews.com/business/software/best-voice-recognition-software/

Quantitative data analysis techniques for data driven marketing

http://tinyurl.com/mb2w6kl

5. Social media and digital scholarship - some critical definitions

It is critical to have a clear understanding of the definitions of social media, scholarship, digital scholarship and digital literacy.

Social media is a subset of applications available on the Internet and the Web which directly facilitates communication between individuals and which generally results in knowledge sharing. Facebook and Twitter are regarded as the two most obvious social media applications. However e-mail itself which is not generally classified as a social media can be used to achieve the same sort of objective. Therefore there is a degree of overlap when it comes to stating which applications should be regarded as social media.

The advantage of using social media is that it is possible to reach a wide audience and therefore give researchers more access to other researchers and potential knowledgeable informants.

Social media may be categorized in several different ways including[2]:

Broadcast v narrowcast,

http://tinyurl.com/gq7ammk

Passive v interactive,

http://tinyurl.com/jcwpg5e

Developmental v disruptive,

http://tinyurl.com/zfs2ygb

Insightful v trivial

http://tinyurl.com/z45zbv4

It is most important to bear in mind that it is a question of perspective as to whether one refers to a system as a social media.

---

[2] Defined and described at the URL quoted below each category.

It is also worth stating that it is still the case that the most popular electronic social medium device is the telephone. In today's environment it would of course be the mobile telephone.

Scholarship may be regarded as being an activity involving being well read and also being able to use such knowledge to create convincing arguments in the scholar's field of interest. Scholarship requires intellectual agility as well as the ability to critique and assemble new concepts and skilfully present them to peers for review and comment. One of the main objectives of academe is to promote scholarship and in so doing to encourage the highest level of academic discourse and achievement from its staff and students.

Scholarship was once thought of as being a relatively solitary endeavour whereby an individual honed his or her skills of understanding a topic and then developed him or herself to be able to make a contribution which would advance the community's understanding of the subject. However, today scholarship is recognised as being an inherently social activity involving a wide range of stakeholders each of whom may have something of direct interest to offer the scholar. One of the key issues in scholarship then becomes how to identify the relevant stakeholders and how to share their thinking on the topic. This may be verbally, or may be in writing or it might be through the medium of producing videos. Thus a variety of different types of communications are a central aspect of successful scholarship and social media are increasingly important.

Digital scholarship refers to the use of the Internet and the Web as well as other electronic tools to facilitate the development of scholarship in individuals.

MIT's Micah Altman on Digital Scholarship
https://www.youtube.com/watch?v=WUhOtdDZWHU

Libraries as collaborators in digital scholarship: Balancing experimentation and sustainability
https://www.youtube.com/watch?v=YF6eUi1VQB4

Digital literacy refers to the level of knowledge of ICT and associated applications required to take advantage of the technology. In the context of academic scholarship digital literacy refers to the type of knowledge which is addressed in this document.

The aim of academic research is to both add something of value to the body of theoretical knowledge and to suggest how such new knowledge may be applied to facilitate the achievement of society's objectives. Academic research is undertaken for the purposes of obtaining a degree or for the publishing of research findings in academic journals. Both of these activities are a fundamental part of career development at a university or a research institute. Of course, other types of research are conducted at universities on behalf of clients such as government, commercial organisations, and professional bodies to mention only a few such entities which may from time to time require research being conducted on their behalf.

6. Strengths, Weaknesses, Opportunities and Threats (SWOT)

Swot analysis is a well established technique for giving a high level overview of a situation and which we are using it here to point out the issues which affect any academic researcher who wishes to use the Internet and the Web to facilitate his or her research.

Strengths: The Internet and the Web is effectively a funnel through which scholars can receive and send information, use tools, communicate, critique, receive assistance, ask questions, watch and listen to experts, publish findings (to gain recognition) and other scholarly activities.

The Internet and the Web expands the reach of scholars in a number of different ways and in so doing provides access to information and individuals on a scale which is actually difficult to describe. In so doing the use of time and other resources can be optimized.

The Internet and the Web has also become important in assisting scholars inform their colleagues, associates, students and the community at large about the results of their research. So the same technology that can facilitate the execution of the research can also help to rapidly disseminate the findings

Those younger researchers who were not active in academic research before the arrival of the Internet sometimes find it difficult to imagine how cumbersome the old systems were and just how much dreary work there was involved in executing an academic research project.

It is correct to say that the Internet and the Web dramatically transformed modern scholarship and in so doing made it much more accessible and it has also raised the level of expectation many academics have for the quality of work which can be provided by their students.

Weaknesses: The providence of material found either through the Internet or on the Web should never be taken at face value. The Internet and the Web provide a unique opportunity for author disguise and this has been exploited by some unscrupulous individuals and therefore care needs to be taken to ensure the authenticity of any information so acquired.

Furthermore the Web can be seen by some students as representing a quick and easy way of producing a dissertation by the cut and paste method. However products such as www.turnitin.com and www.iThenticate.com and www.Grammarly.com can detect such misconduct and plagiarism is no longer the threat to academic integrity it was thought to be a short while ago. Furthermore Turn-it-in has triggered improvements in course and assessment design.

Of course there are still many miscreants who try to cheat in this way and plagiarism remains an unpleasant issue which academic staff has to deal with.

Ghost writing which offers a similar challenge to plagiarism is probably a more pertinent issue because it can be much more difficult to identify and stop than plagiarism. Essays, assignments and dissertations are being written by so-called experts for fees and submitted by students as their own work. Some of the businesses involved in this type of fraud are sufficiently devious to produce work that can escape detection. Only academic faculty's familiarity with the student can reliably catch this type of fraud.

Hoax writing, which is performed by a computer program that can author a paper or an assignment is another threat to academic integrity. These programs were originally created in order to embarrass predatory conferences and journals but they can also fool less attentive academic staff.

Hoax detecting software spots fake papers:
http://tinyurl.com/z3wqn7e

Automated screening: ArXiv screens spot fake paper:
http://tinyurl.com/zw6sazb

Although it is possible to make interesting and useful contacts through electronic means, which will be helpful in various ways it is generally believed that personal face-to-face contact is superior. The likelihood is that whatever form it takes, establishing a network is essentially supportive of the research processes and that it will continue to be a helpful approach to academe and scholarship.

There is another downside issue with regards to using the Internet and the Web and this relates to the fact that once material has been placed on a Website it is not possible to ensure that it will be deleted at a future date if it is no longer required or appropriate to have it there. The suppliers of Web services regularly make backup copies and these copies are stored at various locations around the world and they are not under normal circumstances available to users. It is therefore quite important that no one should ever upload any material which could turn out to be an embarrassment to them in the future. Many university research ethics protocols, insists that the researcher complies with the Data Protection Act, which has provisions concerning the prohibition of data storage in certain parts of the world and the movement of data across certain national boundaries. If the researcher is using a cloud-based system it is impossible for him or her to know where data is being stored and which boundaries the data is crossing.

Websites are being continuously hacked and if researchers use a cloud-based system they will be putting their private details at risk as well as the data they have collected from knowledgeable informants and which they have promised to hold securely.

Opportunities: The main opportunity at present relates to the vast reservoir of information which is available through the Web. It is not possible to know what is actually available on the web either in terms of applications or data. It takes time and effort to explore the Web and even then no one will ever explore more than a small part of it. As many academic researchers need to work to relatively tight schedules there is little time to be distracted by interesting opportunities on the Web that will not necessarily lead to better research. A disciplined approach to the use of the Web is required.

The increasing interest in Data Mining and Big Data and the access to repositories is in its infancy and there will more research opportunities using this type of technology.

The prospects of working across cultures have been improved by language translations facilities which have opened up another spectrum of opportunities.

As previously mentioned it is quite difficult to predict how the Web and the Internet might develop over the next few years. The rate of development of hardware and software is unlikely to slow down and it is most probable that there will be a continuous flow of new ideas as to how to increase work flow efficiency and effectiveness. But the exact nature of these improvements is difficult to forecast.

The trend towards mobile technology will almost certainly continue and therefore scholars will have access to information from wherever they are on a 24/7 basis. It may be expected that the quality of information will improve as both users and suppliers become more mature. However, it is also likely that fraudsters and cheats will also see the Internet as an opportunity and that this type of activity will continue and the scholars need to be on the lookout to protect themselves from this type of misconduct.

Threats: Besides the general problems which everyone who uses the Internet and the Web faces concerning malware and the attempts by fraudsters to embezzle money from unsuspecting users there are a number of particular threats which academic researchers face and about which they have to be constantly vigilant.

At present the threats which the Internet and the Web pose to academe are centred on the way in which it can facilitate dishonesty with regards to academic achievement.

There are also a number of predatory journals and conferences which purport to publish peer reviewed scholarly papers but which actually fail to do even the more elementary reviewing of the papers submitted by the prospective attendees or authors. These organizations take fees from researchers and deliver none of the benefits which they purport to offer. They are a similar manifestation of the phony universities which offer degrees on the basis of only life experiences. The Internet and the Web are also been used to advertise completely fraudulent educational institutions and taking tuition fees from an suspecting individuals and delivering nothing. This type of scam or fraud is usually perpetrated against overseas or foreign students who believe that an attractive website is an indication of an organisation of some substance and some integrity. This of course is not the case and much money has been lost by individuals who have been taken in by attractive advertisements. It is certainly a case of *"caveat emptor"*.

Under this heading of threats it is probably worth mentioning that incidences of cyber bullying at universities have been reported and generally speaking this has to be dealt with and eliminated wherever it occurs. Of course these situations are not easy to handle, but there have been some police prosecutions in recent years and this may help reduce the incidence of this unacceptable form of behaviour.

There is certainly both good and bad to be had from the use of the Internet and Web and it is quite important that users be thoroughly suspicious and do not take anything on face value which they encounter when using these systems. On the other hand, the proper use of the Internet and Web is now almost a sine qua non for success in scholarly research and it is difficult to imagine academic researchers who do not heavily rely of the Internet and the Web.

7. Some most important applications for Digital Scholarship

What any particular researcher considers the most important application available on the Internet and the Web will clearly depend on his or her requirements and their ability to use the software. This is why a significant level of digital literacy is important for academic research in today's environment.

Any application which helps the researcher obtain a better understanding of the research topic may be regarded as an important application or tool. A better understanding of the research topic may be acquired by obtaining more information from the literature or other sources or by facilitating the researcher's ability to network with other knowledgeable individuals who share similar interests.

It is useful to consider applications under 5 categories which are:

1. Research engines
2. Knowledge bases
   a. Encyclopaedia
   b. Libraries including MOOCs
3. Connecting facilities
   a. Off-line and on-line
   b. Real time
4. Utilities
   a. Writing, language, referencing
5. Help
   a. Ask a Librarian

1. Research engines

Information finding tools such as Google, Dogpile, Youtube, and Wikipedia are the first ones to come to the minds of most researchers. These applications can be called everyday tools. It is important not to rely on any one of these, but to use several of them jointly and to check the information found against other sources as there is no guarantee about the accuracy of any information acquired from the Web. It is therefore important to triangulate information by looking at a number of different sources. Never take the veracity of any information found on the Web for granted.

For academic research specialized search engines may be helpful and there are many of these to choose from.

The Top 15 most popular Search Engines

http://www.ebizmba.com/articles/search-engines

A note on Google

Although originally known for its superior search engine, Google is today a multi-technology company specializing in Internet related services and it covers a wide range of issues. Although Google's core product is still their search engine (Google Search) it also offers online productivity software (Google Docs) including e-mail (Gmail), a cloud storage service (Google Drive) and a social networking service (Google+).

In addition to this Google's desktop products include applications for Web browsing (Google Chrome), organizing and editing photos (Google Photos), and instant messaging and video chat (Hangouts).

Google is particularly enthusiastic about its product called Chrome and it is expected that it will continue to strongly encourage users to adopt this as their preferred browser.

http://tinyurl.com/j96efvt

To discuss Chrome there is a chat facility with expert advice at:

http://tinyurl.com/zvhhzrr

Google has developed the Android mobile operating system and the browser-only Chrome OS for a class of Netbooks known as Chromebooks and desktop PCs known as Chromeboxes.

Google has a significant number of additional services, some of which are of direct assistance to academic researchers. There are more than two dozen services and they can be reviewed at

https://www.google.com/intl/en/about/products/

It is worthwhile for the scholar to become familiar with such services.

One service of particular use to academic research is Google books, which allows the user to enter a quotation from a book and the

Google search engine will attempt to identify from which book the quotation comes.

https://books.google.com/?hl=en

2. Knowledge bases

Learning from the body of knowledge - Encyclopaedias

There is an important issue which needs to be addressed early under the heading of important applications and that is the one of Wikipedia. Many academics believe that it is inappropriate for a scholar or even for a research student to cite from either an encyclopaedia or a dictionary as a reference in formal academic writing. There is no solid reason for this other than the assumption that those who are writing as well as those who are reading a formal peace of academic work should be fully familiar with the level of information which can be supplied by a popular publication such as an encyclopaedia or a dictionary.

Specifically on the question of Wikipedia academics have turned their faces against this Web-based publication, mostly because it is crowd sourced and thus anyone can develop entries or add information to its pages. Wikipedia does provide some curation, but it is generally believed that it does not prevent either errors of fact or distortions due to the bias of the contributors from being included in the entries into this encyclopaedia. In defence of Wikipedia the management points out that there have always been errors in encyclopaedias and they claim that there are no more errors in Wikipedia than in the Encyclopaedia Britannica.

From the point of view of academic research Wikipedia is an invaluable resource from which it is possible to obtain a summary overview of a subject area. In addition, many Wikipedia entries provide a list of references and for many this is a useful starting point from which to pursue a literature review. It is recommended that this website be used freely in this respect.

However, it is important to note that at the present time in most circumstances, citing Wikipedia as a source in a formal academic document would be considered inappropriate.

There are other encyclopaedias, some of which are open access, on the Web and these include:

http://www.encyclopedia.com/

http://www.libraryspot.com/encyclopedias.htm

http://www.thefreedictionary.com/

Other Links relating to encyclopaedias:

Open Access Encyclopaedias:

https://www.insidehighered.com/news/2009/12/14/encyclopedias

Writing an Open Accessed Encyclopaedia in a Closed Accessed World:

http://tinyurl.com/jvblrfv

Learning from the world with MOOCs

A MOOC is a Massive Open Online Course which delivers specialised information in the form of a lecture or a series of lectures. It is sometimes but not always accompanied by tests and the submission of assignments.

https://en.wikipedia.org/wiki/Massive_open_online_course

There are MOOCs which provide a substantial amount of information to facilitate a novice researcher coming to grips with many of the core issues of academic research. Youtube and TED.COM and be helpful in this respect.

Academicearth is a website that represents a collection of university courses, which include many of the most highly rated universities in the world:

http://academicearth.org/

Academicearth is a particularly interesting application where full courses in a wide range of subjects may be observed and listened to by anyone from anywhere in the world. In general these courses do not include any interaction between the faculty and the observer/listener. There is some controversy about whether a Website such as academicearth.org actually constitutes a MOOC and it may be appropriate to talk about a full MOOC and a partial MOOC. The difference lies in the use of the word course. At Academicearth anyone may observe some of the best university courses at Harvard, Princeton, Yale or UCLA. But these do not have any ability to give the observer/listener the opportunity to communicate with the instructors. It has been argued that if one can only observe then it is not a proper course. If that view is taken then only situations where the observer can submit work to be reviewed and evaluated should be described as a MOOC.

There is a substantial list of MOOCs available on the Web at

https://www.mooc-list.com/

http://www.mooc.ca/providers.htm

3. Connecting facilities

With regards to networking with other knowledgeable individuals, after finding people though Web searches and making contact through e-mail, video conferencing tools are the next step with which to start a dialogue. Skype and as mentioned above Google's Hangouts are the first step in this respect.

But there are a number of other applications including:

http://www.rhubcom.com/v5/video-conferencing.html

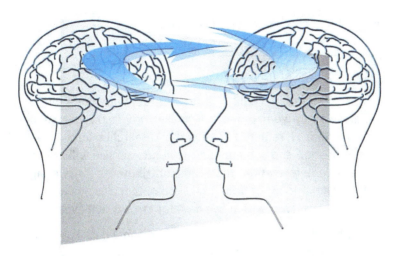

An important issue is the variability in the quality of the transmission and the reception. On occasions, all parties involved can experience almost perfect transmission and reception. Unfortunately this is not always the case and at times the broadband connection can be so poor to make the use of this technology inappropriate.

Connecting for collaboration

Another way of understanding social media is that it represents a set of applications which allows academic researchers to collaborate. The most important application is probably still e-mail, but products like Facebook and Twitter have been given high prominence in this respect and these will be discussed in detail later in the book.

4. Utilities

See section 19 of this book for a section devoted to Utilities.

5. Help

There is a service in both the United Kingdom and the United States of America whereby librarians are prepared to pick up questions and help find appropriate information for the questioner.

This is the free service called Ask a Librarian:

http://www.nls.uk/contact/ask-a-librarian

https://info.askalibrarian.org/

The Ask a Librarian facility varies a little depending on which librarian picks up your request. However, in general the service is useful. All that is required is that the researcher keys in a well-defined question and someone in the library service will attempt to find suitable information that can contribute to answering the question. The amount of time it takes to obtain a reply varies, but it seems that an answer within five days is normally achieved.

Some although not all librarians supply personal details so that the researcher can follow up on an answer and ask for further explanations, however, some don't.

It is hard to overestimate the importance of YouTube as a source of useful information for any researcher. Like Wikipedia it is not regarded as being appropriately authenticated to be used as a formal reference. However some of the material available through YouTube is useful as a first step in researching a topic. Interesting examples of such videos are supplied below and these address basic issues related to the nature of academic research and also how important it is for the researcher to be clear that he or she shares the same vocabulary as any informant which they intend to employ.

The Illusion of Truth (A Youtube video which discusses and demonstrates at a practical level whether if you repeat something enough times, it comes to feel good and true.)

https://www.youtube.com/watch?v=cebFWOlx848

What is a photocopier (A humorous Youtube video highlighting the necessity for defining terms and clarifying your questions in any research interview)

https://www.youtube.com/watch?v=PZbqAMEwtOE

8. Intellectual Property Rights

The issue of copyright has become more important as more publishers are requiring authors and researchers to seek permission before direct quotations may be used from already published works. This is especially important if the researcher wishes to use a diagram, a drawing or a photograph.

Copyright law varies from country to country. In the United Kingdom, text and images are protected by copyright legislation for 75 years after the death of the author or the artist. The number of years protection varies from country to country and researchers wishing to use material from abroad should become familiar with the regulations of the country of origin of the material.

In using Web resources it cannot be assumed that the reader of any text or the viewer of any video has an automatic right to use it in their work. The intellectual property rights of the creator of the material should be respected at all times. This means that on many occasions it will be necessary to obtain permission to use any material directly in a dissertation or in an academic paper. If the material is not used directly, but has influenced the thinking of the researcher a traditional reference will normally be adequate. There are special rules for referencing Web-based material and researchers need to become familiar with these. If drawings and photographs are used, then it is particularly important to obtain permission from the originator. Wiki Commons and Pixabay provide some pictures and drawings which may be used without specific permissions.

Wiki Commons

www.commons.wikimedia.org is a free of charge media repository of pictures and videos which may be used without having to acquire any further permission from their creators. It is a particularly useful source of images which may be used to illustrate academic texts.

www.pixabay.com

This Website offers both free and paid for access to images.

More paid for images may be found at

http://tinyurl.com/zhty9kt

Creative Commons

In addition to the sharing of images there are also significant repositories of other types of work, including text and slides and videos.

Some interesting sources

https://creativecommons.org/

http://www.slideshare.net/

http://tinyurl.com/cqhq9v6

Material found through Creative Commons should be indicated with the CC mark.

Creating an article on Wikipedia

There is a substantial set of guidelines provided on the Web by Wikipedia to be used in creating an entry for the encyclopaedia. It is a good exercise for researchers to create articles for the encyclopaedia on topics related to the research question and the methods they are going to use in answering the research question.

See:

https://en.wikipedia.org/wiki/Wikipedia:Your_first_article

A research focus only

As previously mentioned this book focuses on how the Internet and the Web impact academic research and has deliberately omitted issues related to using this technology for teaching in higher educational institutions. Looking at how digital technology has affected research is a vast enough topic on its own for any book. However it is worth mentioning that there are many academics who believe that the impact of this technology on academic teaching and administration will end up by being far greater than it has been and is likely to be on research practices.

The subject of how the Internet and the Web have impacted teaching is generally described by the term e-Learning which appears to have been adopted by most institutions to some extent and is used extensively by a smaller number. E-Learning not only gives higher educational institutions a far greater reach than ever before but it also allows them to have much more control over teaching processes as well as provides an extensive platform for being able to administer the entire life-cycle of study of any student. The topic of e-Learning is of course extensively written about in its own right.

9. Incorporating social media and digital scholarship into a research design

A research design is a cornerstone of any research project and needs to be given considerable thought before any development work towards answering the research question should commence.

A research design reflects, or rather is built upon, the philosophical orientation of the researcher. In research jargon this means that the research design incorporates or is developed from the ontological and epistemological view of the researcher. There are in fact only a small number of philosophical stances which may be followed in academic research and researchers need to be fully familiar with what these mean and what the implications are choosing when a particular option. Each stance will lead to a particular methodological approach. The diagram below indicates the main methodologies available to academic researchers.

Theoretical   Empirical

Positivist –   Interpretivist
little i
                   – large I

Non-Empirical   Mixed Methods

Critical Theory   Critical Realism

Design and Construction Science

There is much written material on the Web concerning these research methodological issues and there is also a large number of presentations available through YouTube. Researchers will find some of these useful.

Some Youtube presentations:

https://www.youtube.com/watch?v=GYywR7SA03E

https://www.youtube.com/watch?v=oNpA-joyuZY

https://www.youtube.com/watch?v=hCOsY5rkRs8

https://www.youtube.com/watch?v=l6ZoCuzixao

https://www.youtube.com/watch?v=4NQHeI8GD54

https://www.youtube.com/watch?v=iWnA7nZO4EY

The first step in a research design is to create a high level plan which explicitly articulates whether the work will be based on a theoretical approach or empirical research or research informed by Critical Theory. Within the category of empirical research there is the choice of quantitative, qualitative or mixed methods.

Then the design will address issues such as the actual methods of data collection, analysis and the presentation of the findings. A research design has to be cogniscent of the resources available to the researcher and the time in which the research needs to be completed.

The Internet and Web facilitates theoretical research by providing easier access to literature and by making video conferencing available so that a researcher can enter into dialogue with other researchers around the world.

Both quantitative and qualitative research can be further facilitated through the Internet and the Web by using it to make contact, not only with other researchers, but also with appropriate knowledgeable informants around the world. This will be discussed further under the headings of Facebook and Twitter.

Mixed methods is of increasing importance in research design and a leading authority on this approach to research has an instructive video on Youtube at:

https://www.youtube.com/watch?v=1OaNiTlpyX8

Top 15 Qualitative Data Analysis Software:

http://tinyurl.com/h2kvbbv

Software for Quantitative Research:

http://atlasti.com/quantitative-software/

10. Fast tracking the literature review by identifying the most important papers

The extant literature is the fundamental cornerstone of all academic research and thus it is essential that this activity be undertaken thoroughly. It is important to understand the dual purpose of a literature review, which is for the academic researcher to establish what is already known about the proposed research topic as well, as to obtain an understanding of how this topic has been previously researched. Traditionally literature reviews were entirely based on published text (preferably from peer reviewed academic journals), but increasingly due to the wide availability of video material on academic topics it is possible to obtain considerable depth of understanding from non-text sources. YouTube is a good example of where interesting material may be found. However, as previous mentioned many academics would not yet be prepared to accept citations which exclusively relied on this type of material as part of formal academic writing.

Fast tracking a literature review means being focused on the topic of the research and seeking out the most relevant papers which throws light on the research question and possible answers.

A structured literature review (SLR), accompanied by a literature review map is a relatively new approach to demonstrating how previous research inter-connects and how the researchers thinking has developed throughout the literature review process.

A useful paper on this is available at:

http://files.eric.ed.gov/fulltext/ED505733.pdf

Google Scholar is for most purposes a suitable place to start any literature review. In addition, most universities will have the online research facilities and these will give academic researchers easy access to published materials. These private search facilities are sometimes referred to as the Deep Web because they are not available to the general public. For novice researchers it is recommended that they conduct this type of literature search with the assistance of a librarian.

With a literature review it is essential to locate the most important papers on the topic. One criterion for establishing the importance of a paper is to find out how frequently it has been cited in other works. Highly cited papers should be given prominence. For this the Google citation monitoring facility is useful.

A quick guide on how to use Google's citation service:

https://www.youtube.com/watch?v=_gH5kjVtc1o

Writing a Literature Review (an overview and guide):

http://writingcenter.unc.edu/handouts/literature-reviews/

Short sharp Literature Review principles:

http://guides.library.ucsc.edu/write-a-literature-review

Who is worth reading?

www.harzing.com

Paid for academic research database:

https://www.questia.com

MARS-Mobile Academic Research Support for iPhone:

http://tinyurl.com/jjony6v

Dark Web – what is it and how to access it:

https://darkWebnews.com/help-advice/access-dark-Web/

Fast-track Peer Review – what is it and does it help the researcher?

http://tinyurl.com/hl4y9bs

How to increase citations to your published work

https://www.youtube.com/watch?v=Jld3sV5fd68

Tips from a journal editor: How to select a journal for your paper?

https://www.youtube.com/watch?v=-WBTL8PAv2o

The H-Index

The H index is a metric which is intended to measure an author's productivity and publication impact as a cited scholar. This index is calculated by establishing a set of the authors most cited published papers and then counting the number of citations these papers have received in the work of other scholars. This index was suggested by Jorge Hirsch in 2005.

http://tinyurl.com/jvolxp4

The G-Index

the G-index is an alternative to the H index which does not average the number of citations received by a particular scholar and therefore normally provides a higher score than the H-index.

http://www.benchfly.com/blog/h-index-what-it-is-and-how-to-find-yours/

11. Research question development

Most aspects of academic research benefit from different opinions being taken into account. The Internet and Web can facilitate this in different ways besides that of videoconferencing, which has been mentioned earlier.

In the first instance there are Virtual Notice Boards, sometimes called Bulletin Boards on which announcements may be made and where replies can be received.

A list of some of these is available at:

http://tinyurl.com/7cd8jcl

Then there is Facebook where a researcher may set up a page for a topic and make comments and receive replies. The success of this is entirely dependent on the researcher network. The research needs to be able to announce the existence of the Facebook page to a substantial body of colleagues and associates in order to spark a discussion. If this succeeds, it is a useful way of refining a research question.

A similar effect can be achieved by creating a blog. Blogs are relatively easy to set up, but the difficulty is in attracting enough attention from interested people.

A blog which may be worth looking at

http://danremenyi-research-methology.blogspot.co.uk/

At the time of writing this blog has received a large number of viewers but not many have contributed to a discussion.

A quick and easy approach to setting up a blog is provided by

https://edublogs.org/

There are several applications which should be considered when selecting a system with which to create a blog including:

https://www.blogger.com/home?bpli=1&pli=1

Attracting visitors/readers and then encouraging contributions to a discussion is the main issue and is not easy. The researcher needs to continually invite readers and set up notifications when the blog is updated. In addition to written blogs there is also the possibility of using video blogs (sometimes referred to as Vlogs).

For information on Vlogs see:

http://tinyurl.com/zdsogow

It may be relevant to use Twitter in order to establish whether there is already some debate on the topic you wish to discuss. If this is the case, it may be possible to plug into an already established debate or to find potentially interested people through their Tweets.

Facebook is widely understood to be the largest social media platform available with approx. 1.1 billion monthly active users. It allows its users to have "friends" on their profile with whom they can share photos, videos, links, instant messaging and more, and a profile can be created quickly and for free using an existing email address.

Whilst many people are aware of Facebook they may not know how to use it as a research tool. Like Twitter, Facebook uses hashtags which will inform the user what is "trending", and will broadcast information from a wide range of high-profile actors and companies.

A unique and appealing aspect of Facebook is its groups, which are not a feature on Twitter. A group on Facebook is a page where people can join to discuss a particular topic of interest. These groups may be open or closed; if the group is closed by the administrator (who set up the group) he or she will need to accept a request to join.

There are many groups with the focus of Social Media Research

https://www.facebook.com/search/groups/?q=social%20media%20research

It is possible to set up your own group or groups and invite individuals from your friend list to join it. If the group is public individuals who are not Facebook users may be able to view the

page, but not actively engage with the content. It is important to note that setting up a group does not require an individual to have an established network of friends on Facebook.

Throughout universities these groups are commonly set up and used by students to discuss and share materials with their peers. They are also an easy way to identify people who may be valuable participants in your research. Furthermore, due to the reach of Facebook as a social media platform even demographics which are underrepresented within the 1.1 billion monthly active uses may still be available in very large numbers.

On Facebook it is normally not considered etiquette to send individuals you do not know in real life friend requests. However it is acceptable to join groups set up by and comprised of people who the researcher may not actually know

NB: Describing Facebook as a social media application is quite similar to seeing a telephone as a social media application in as far as a telephone allows the user to reach out to a large group of people and attempt to engage in a dialogue with them. But just like the telephone it is of little use, unless its owner has a long list of acquaintances that are prepared to talk to him or to her. A Facebook group requires the user to develop a set of acquaintances that are prepared to engage in the type of discussion that is required. Depending on the researchers' circumstances it may not be that difficult to develop such a group, but it is seldom that this can be done quickly and therefore the researcher needs to plan the development of his or her own group or network, somewhat in advance of needing to use it.

The Google Corporation launched its equivalent of Facebook which it called Google+ in 2011. Its offering is similar to Facebook. Because of Google's market place power it has a substantial number of users but it does not seem to have taken market share from Facebook.

12. Identifying and working with knowledgeable informants

Besides Facebook there are two other important applications which need to be considered and these are Twitter® and LinkedIn®.

Twitter is a tool to identify valuable potential informants.

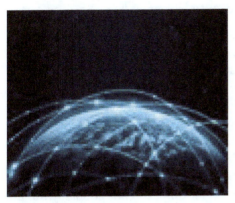

Twitter is an online social media platform developed in 2006 that has a significant number of users (estimated at 313 million active monthly users), who could be useful to the researcher. Twitter is free to use and it can be signed up to relatively easily using an existing email address. Twitter allows individuals or organisations to broadcast messages up to 140 characters to their followers. Followers are people who have chosen to receive other people's Twitter updates on their personal timeline. High profile accounts may have a blue tick next to their names; this means they are 'verified'. Verified accounts often belong to high-profile actors or politicians.

Twitter is not only a platform for individuals, as increasingly organizations and businesses are using twitter as a communications tool. Be aware that twitter allows individuals to customise their privacy settings to varying degrees. High profile people and organisations will usually be very public, whereas other people may wish be much more private. Private accounts cannot be engaged with until a request is made to follow them, and this request has been accepted by the owner of the account. It is deemed socially acceptable to follow individuals on Twitter who the researcher may not know, even if their accounts are private, in a way which is not so accepted on platforms such as Facebook.

There are a number of ways to find people on Twitter who can be useful to a research project. Firstly, Twitter's own search engine can be used. This search engine can search tweets, accounts, photos, videos or news.

Advanced search can be used to narrow down results by date and location.

https://twitter.com/search-advanced?lang=en-gb

Searching Twitter using a hashtag (#) can be a useful way to identify individuals exchanging views about a topic. Hashtags are any given string of characters with a special character (#) in front of it and when they are clicked on, one can see other tweets include this hashtag for example #socialmedia and #digitalscholarship. Anyone can create and use a hashtag. Popular ones that are being used at any given moment can be found in Twitters 'Trends', which lists what is being extensively used at that time. Top trends are often related to big public events, i.e. football matches, earthquakes and elections. If the researcher is seeking to find people who are discussing topics relevant to their research, they can search their topic as a hashtag to see who is communicating about it. For instance #SocialMediaResearch is a hashtag that has been widely used and may be of some interest. Not only does this identify people who are talking about Social Media Research, but it is possible to also source new information and articles through this method. Although Twitter restricts Tweets to 140 characters, it is possible to include links. It is important to note that hashtags can also be used on other platforms, notably Facebook and Instagram. Their use is more widespread and thus more useful on Twitter.

Once relevant informants have been identified on Twitter it is possible to view who they follow, who follows them, tweets they have liked and who they have been tweeting. This is interesting to remember, as the researcher may be able to identify and communicate with more relevant people through viewing these.

Messages sent on Twitter have been used as a source of secondary data and academic researchers have used the Tweets of others as the raw material for their analysis.

There is some debate as to whether these Tweets may be regarded as secondary data.

http://tinyurl.com/pd6u94a

Research based on this approach may need specific authorization from the university ethics committee. This was well described by Paul and Dredze (2016), who said

> *Twitter, Facebook and other social media encourage frequent user expressions of their thoughts, opinions and random details of their lives. Tweets and status updates range from important events to inane comments. Most messages contain little informational value but the aggregation of millions of messages can generate important knowledge. Several Twitter studies have demonstrated that aggregating millions of messages can provide valuable insights into a population.*

Useful utilities include

https://blog.twitter.com/2015/welcome-to-twitter-data

http://mozdeh.wlv.ac.uk/installation.html

http://lexiurl.wlv.ac.uk/

http://nodexl.codeplex.com/

A caveat to using Twitter:

The demographics of Twitter users may not represent the types of knowledgeable informants which are required to answer a particular research question.

Twitter users tend to be young and for academic research they may not have the amount of experience which is required for an individual to be regarded as a suitable knowledgeable informant.

It is easy to be overwhelmed by the number of potential contacts that can be offered by the use of Twitter. Data Deluge is a term used to describe more data than can be easily handled. However although it may appear that there is a huge amount of data available often only a very small amount of it is actually useful.

Trolling

The nature of Twitter is that it is open to anyone and some individuals who tweet may be exceptionally crass and rude. There is also a phenomenon called 'trolling'. Trollers make abusive and or threatening remarks often using fake accounts so that they cannot be identified. It can be very disturbing. If trolls are encountered they should be reported to the authorities.

Linkedin®

The career professional equivalent of Facebook is Linkedin.

http://www.linkedin.com

Whereas Facebook was initially designed for social exchanges between friends, LinkedIn was created in order to allow professional individuals to contact with each other in the context of enhancing their career prospects. It is estimated to have about 430 million registers members of which 100 million are said to be active. It is available in over 20 different languages. In 2012 the Linkedin Website was hacked and user passwords were stolen. Linkedin asked its users to change their passwords.

Linkedin offers various paid for services.

In most respects LinkedIn may be used by academic researchers in the same way as they would use Facebook.

More academic contacts

Twitter and LinkedIn are especially useful in making contacts with knowledgeable informants who will offer data which may be used in the academic research process. It is of considerable importance for academic researchers to make contacts with as wide a range of potential informants and other stakeholders though out the research.

13.   Data capture using social media

The data required by academic researchers is often described as originating from two sources, which are said to be either primary data or secondary data. Primary data is defined as data obtained by the researcher for the purposes of the research project through some sort of observation, which includes but is of course not limited to seeing and listening or reading the replies given to questions. Secondary data on the other hand, is data, which has already been collected and published for some other reason than answering the current research question and which the researcher finds appropriate to facilitate his or her understanding and answering of the research question.

There are many different sources of primary data, which include data obtained from recording the results of experiments, data obtained from interviews, data obtained from questionnaires, data obtained from personal and corporate documents. In the social science world the most common forms of data are acquired from interviewing, focus groups, questionnaires and from extant documents.

Interviewing is essentially a face-to-face activity which has traditionally been performed by an interviewer and an informant in the same location. The Internet and Web has facilitated interviewing by making available video conferencing.

Videoconferencing can be a suitable substitute and thus save considerable travel expense and time. As already mentioned www.Skype.com and Google Hangouts https://hangouts.google.com/ are among the most popular. However, videoconferencing is highly dependent on the quality of the broadband connection available. As sometimes this can be poor it may be necessary to reschedule interviews, when there is a better connection available.

With regards to questionnaires the Internet and the Web have simplified both their creation of questionnaires and their dissemination. Also the same software can also in some cases facilitate the analysis of the data.

The dominant software for questionnaire development

https://www.surveymonkey.com/

but

https://www.qualtrics.com/

is considered by many to have more facilities.

Within the Google suite of software, there is a product which is referred to as Google Forms which provides a facility for creating questionnaires online. It is another important product which has the advantage that it easily interfaces into Google software which provides analytical capability.

Guidelines for Web based questionnaire design

http://lap.umd.edu/survey_design/questionnaires.html

Comments of questionnaires

http://www.simplypsychology.org/questionnaires.html

Integrated questionnaire system

https://www.questionpro.com/Web-survey.html

It is also possible to set up Focus Groups on the Web.

Information of a text based Focus Group may be found at

http://e-focusgroups.com/online.html

Another way of thinking about the Web is that may be viewed as the largest repository of secondary data in the world and as such it is a treasure trove to all academic researchers. Secondary data is always of great importance to the academic researcher and thus the Web's role as a provider of this data should not be underrated.

The key issue is to what extent can the data obtained from Web sources be regarded as reliable. There is no simple answer to this question. Some parts of the Web represent the most reliable information available anywhere. Other parts have been created by those with absolutely no interest in providing authentic or accurate information.

It is always the researcher's responsibility to ensure the integrity of whatever data, he or she uses and therefore considerable care has to be taken when using any information found on the Web. This has already been referred to when discussing Wikipedia and YouTube. Any information which the researcher finds on the Web, and which he or she intends to rely on as important evidence in the research should be, at a minimum, triangulated. This means confirming the information with whatever other sources there may be available for this purpose.

14. Tools for quantitative and qualitative data analysis

As pointed out in an earlier section there are many software products available for data analysis but most of these tend to be installed applications and not freely available through the Web. However, the Web is an excellent way of finding appropriate data and finding reviews on different products. It should therefore be seen as a repository of information about these tools rather than a source of the tools themselves.

On the other hand, there are some applications available on the Web which themselves can be directly useful to the researcher in the analysis of data. One of these is Google Forms which allows both questionnaires to be developed anglicised.

21 free qualitative data analysis products some of which are available on the Web:

http://tinyurl.com/o8bs69j

There are numerous tutorials on Youtube for various statistical packages including:

SPSS for beginners

https://www.youtube.com/watch?v=ADDR3_Ng5CA

Using SAS

http://tinyurl.com/q2ghxva

An introduction to R

https://www.youtube.com/watch?v=LjuXiBjxryQ

For qualitative data analysis see:

NVIVO

http://tinyurl.com/q2ghxva

Introduction to ATLAS ti

https://www.youtube.com/watch?v=Fko3eQ6Q_Qc

Links to further information

Reframer is a qualitative research tool designed to improve the traceability of qualitative research, the discovery of patterns and themes, and the effectiveness of a team:

http://tinyurl.com/z6rdv3p

Jmp Statistical Discovery offers interactive statistical analysis:

http://tinyurl.com/z7vze2y

15. The implications of social media on research ethics protocols

Researchers should not assume that the use of social media as an integral part of their research design will be welcomed by the university ethics authorities. The thinking of ethics committees can be less advanced and less informed than leading edge ideas concerning how to facilitate researchers.

Although concern for ethics in non-medical academic research is a relatively recent phenomenon universities are increasingly concerned about ethical issues related to the conduct of academic research. This has resulted in research projects that directly or indirectly involve human participation requiring approval by university ethics committees. The purpose of this is to ensure that all academic researchers are fully familiar with what is considered to be good research practice and that they avoid any harm coming to those who participate in the research and that they do nothing to put at risk the good name of the University.

In general, this requires a research project to be fully planned before it begins and for the researcher to closely comply with the plans which have been approved. Unfortunately, this does tend to restrict the researcher and can limit the extent to which the research evolves as a result of new opportunities that develop along the way. Of course each University will differ in this respect and the researcher needs to be clear on precisely what is allowed by his or her institution.

It is particularly important to note that anyone who contributes to research data should have given the researcher his/her Informed Consent before the data can be used. It is also important that the researcher makes every effort to anonymise data and to ensure that if the data is supplied confidentially, this is fully respected.

Where possible informed consent should be obtained in writing. It is possible to design a measuring instrument, such as a questionnaire in such a way that if it is completed by an informant he or she will have ipso facto provided informed consent to the researcher. If this technique is used the ethics approval committee needs to authorise it in advance.

Once informants' data has been collected the researcher becomes a custodian of that data whilst it is required for the research and once the research has been completed it is incumbent upon the researcher to ensure that the data is eventually destroyed. The amount of time the researcher needs to retain the data will vary from University to University.

As mentioned before one issue which arises through the use of the Web to store informants' data is that the Data Protection Act in the UK specifies regulations concerning cross-border movement of data. It also provides rules concerning in which countries it is acceptable to have data stored. If researchers are using cloud-based repositories for their data it may not be possible for them to know where the data is located and which national boundaries the transmission of the data has crossed. It is therefore quite possible for an academic researcher to inadvertently infringe the Data Protection Act, which could bring him or her into conflict with the University.

https://www.gov.uk/data-protection/the-data-protection-act

Links to further information

What is Ethics in Research & Why is it Important?

https://www.niehs.nih.gov/research/resources/bioethics/whatis/

Ethics in research

https://explorable.com/ethics-in-research

Research ethics

https://www.youtube.com/watch?v=Zbi7nIbAuMQ

Research ethics involving human subjects

https://www.youtube.com/watch?v=-O5gsF5oyls

The ethics of social research

https://www.youtube.com/watch?v=BQeUuxIzsfU

16. Support for research processes

The work performed in a major academic research project should be meticulously logged. This gives the researchers oversight of what has been done and therefore the possibility of some control over the project as it is unfolding and also it provide a written record of the project which may be useful if the researcher wants to produce an audit trail at the end of the work. Although these details could be kept in Word or some other word processing package there is also a logging or diary facility in Microsoft Outlook.

Specialised Web based diaries are plentiful and inexpensive.

Top 7 free websites with which to keep an on-line diary

http://tinyurl.com/gshrgsn

Other diary websites

https://www.myoffice.net/onlinediaries.aspx?source=WebDiaries

http://www.diaroapp.com/

However there is much more to managing a research project than simply keeping a diary.

Every academic research project will have its own individual research processes. However, all academic research projects may be considered to have five macro-processes:

- establishing the research question and positioning it within the extant literature;
- selecting an appropriate research methodology using suitable research methods;
- conducting the research;
- analysing and interpreting the findings;
- concluding the research with comments on its application and on its limitations.

These processes can be facilitated by the use of appropriate project management and workflow software. In fact any sizeable research project of size which is intended to stay within the original time frame will need the facilities which are offered by this type of software product if it is to be conducted efficiently and effectively.

The standard project management techniques of network diagrams and bar charts can be helpful in both planning and supporting an academic research project, and researchers should take time to understand how these techniques work. It is possible to acquire dedicated software to produce such diagrams, but it is equally possible to use a product such as Excel to monitor an academic project.

Links to further information

http://tinyurl.com/hokkdq3

http://tinyurl.com/hlrcpd8

17. Dissemination of research findings and establishing an academic reputation

There are two major aspects to academic research which go hand-in-hand, but which are not always clearly separated. The first of these is that the objective of academic research is to produce new knowledge. Stated formally academic research is required to add something of value to the body of theoretical knowledge. The second issue is that this new knowledge needs to be made available to the community in which the researchers live and work. There are two reasons why dissemination is important. In the first place most universities are public institutions funded by the State and therefore research findings need to be made known to members of the public in the expectation that they will be of some use to them. The second point is that academics need to receive personal recognition for the research work they have undertaken. Credit for the research leads to confirmation of their positions at the university and perhaps even to promotion.

This dissemination of research findings has always been an important dimension of a scholar's work and has typically not been adequately emphasised. In general, academics have been much better at the creation of knowledge than at its dissemination. The principal means by which knowledge has been disseminated has been through publication in academic or scientific journals. These journals have established strict rules which have helped to ensure that authentic research as opposed to pseudo-research is published. However, being published in an academic journal has been an imperfect process, and there are examples of inappropriate material being published as well as good material being ignored.

The Web on the Internet has opened up opportunities for scholars to be published in other ways than through the established academic or scientific journals.

There are a number of options. Firstly, research findings may be published in departmental or university repositories. This is a useful first step in giving the research some visibility. Secondly, there are a number of repositories where research findings may be uploaded. Examples are discussed in detail later. This serves as a form of publishing, albeit digital. Thirdly, researchers can create their own Websites and have their research findings and papers accessible through these. Researchers can create videos about their research and their findings and have these uploaded on YouTube.

Many universities are helping in this respect, and a number of academic libraries are actively involved in building institutional repositories to include all the research activities on their campus. These institutional repositories (IRs) are online archives for collecting, preserving, and disseminating digital copies of the intellectual output of the institution. Universities are increasingly encouraging of researchers using their website to display their research.

Many of these repositories are made available to the general public with few restrictions, in accordance with the goals of open access, in contrast to the publication of research in paid for (commercial) journals, where the publishers often limit access rights through the imposition of high costs of purchase. Institutional, truly free, and corporate repositories are sometimes referred to as digital libraries (DL).

D-Lib Magazine – The magazine of digital library research:

http://www.dlib.org/dlib/july16/07contents.html

In addition to this some academics are also publishing their own dissertations, text books and monographs through print-on-demand organizations. This can be inexpensive and effective in disseminating their ideas to students and colleagues.

A print-on-demand market leader

http://www.ingramcontent.com/publishers

Furthermore there is the communication of research, both complete and work-in-progress through a number of academic networking sites such as www.researchgate.net and https://www.academia.edu/ which allow scholars to inform their communities of the latest research which has been undertaken. More will be said about this under points of general interest.

For scholars who are already published there is a potential income stream to be obtained if they register with the Authors' Licensing and Collecting Society.

www.alcs.co.uk/

Academic researchers need to establish for themselves a reputation within the wider community.

Three important Websites in this respect are

http://www.Academia.edu

It is a repository of publications where academic researchers may upload their work and thus allow it to be accessed by others. It is most useful for facilitating the receipt of academic material from collaborators.

A series of analytics are provided so that the researcher can keep track of that interest that has been shown in his or her work and where geographically the interested parties are from. This website also invites scholars to submit a draft paper on which they might like to have some feedback.

https://www.researchgate.net/home

This is described as a social networking site for researchers to share information including papers, to pose and answer questions, and to find collaborators. According to Nature and it is the largest academic social network in terms of active users.

ResearchGate requires the user to keep a database of his or her published work and to be prepared to send copies of papers to academics who request them. This website keeps a record of how many people are reading which papers and how frequently papers are being cited. It can certainly improve an academics' visibility within the community of scholars. It also has a means by which academics can endorse other academics for particular skill sets. Job opportunities are also presented on its Web pages.

https://www.mendeley.com/

Mendeley offers a comprehensive set of services to scholars including a paper repository, networking and brainstorming opportunities to mention only a few of its facilities.

It also is a reference management system which was acquired by the large international publisher Elsevier.

Links to further information

Academic networks contest: ResearchGate vs. Academia vs. Mendeley

http://tinyurl.com/zmqowje

18. The Cloud

It is important for all scholars to understand the implications of the cloud which has become a fundamental part of nearly all computing architecture. Cloud computing simply means network computing. It is said that the origins of the term are unclear, but for many years computer analysts and programmers used a cloud shape in systems diagrams to signify connections between computers which relied on a data communications network.

Today the term cloud refers to the global network of hardware, software and telecommunications devices on which the Internet and the Web functions, as well as all the user orientated facilities which can be accessed through this global network.

The cloud is truly ubiquitous. Whenever anyone uses Google or any other search engine the communication is over the cloud. When e-mail is sent it will be stored somewhere in the world and the location of this will be determined by software and hardware which will be intrinsic parts of the cloud.

So at this level cloud computing is now inescapable. Only the most local computing to do work such as writing a letter or producing a report or creating a set of presentation slides which would be printed out in the office would avoid using the cloud.

But there is much more to this issue than search engines and e-mail and this relates to whether a computer user purchases hardware and software to perform regularly data processing tasks on his or her own computer or whether he or she rents or subscribes to software and hardware (normally Storage) from a cloud supplier.

There are financial advantages and disadvantages to both of these options but these are not of concern to the issue of scholarship. The main issue which should exercise scholars is that of security. If data is stored on a personal computing device in the possession of a scholar then he or she has direct control over it. If data is stored in the cloud then control has been surrendered to the service provider. Cloud service vendors are intensely aware of security issues and their systems to protect the data are generally robust but nonetheless it is not uncommon to hear of hackers breaking into cloud based systems. It is much more difficult for a hacker to break into a hard disk on the scholar's desk or into a memory stick which is in the scholar's desk drawer.

It is useful to follow the advice of data security websites such as

http://www.protectyourdata.ca/en/protect-your-data/

http://tinyurl.com/gpdz4fw

Another important issue regarding using the cloud is that anything which is transmitted or stored on the cloud will probably remain there indefinitely. Because the Internet and the Web are vulnerable to hackers the suppliers of these services arrange regular backup copies. Once a data item has been backed up and inserted in an achieve it is not possible to be certain that any steps a user takes will lead to its complete deletion. For this reason great care has to be taken not to write anything which might at a future date be seen as inappropriate. The rules of are clear on this point.

http://tinyurl.com/gwnupl8

https://en.wikipedia.org/wiki/Etiquette_in_technology

Finally as mentioned before the way that cloud service providers arrange their data storage procedures and the countries which they select for this function may not comply with the Data Protection Act. And even if it appears that there is no problem at the outset of a project there will never be a guarantee that the data storage and transmission arranges won't change.

Information about the Data Protection Act is available at

https://ico.org.uk/for-the-public/

This does not mean that a researcher should not use any cloud facilities, but it is important for all researchers to know the inherent challenges which this technology can offer academic research, especially with regards the university's research ethics requirements.

Links to further information

https://en.wikipedia.org/wiki/Cloud_computing

http://tinyurl.com/6ycnd9c

19. Utilities

From the point of view of an academic researcher there are many utilities available on the Web. These range from software which facilitates the sharing of ideas among researchers to referencing tutorials, to language translation, to managing references to mention only a few.

For note taking

https://evernote.com/

For managing referencing

https://endnote.com/

Tracking citations

A number of utilities are available which help with tracking scholars levels of citations. One of the most popular of these is www.harzing.com. Note that care is to be taken when using this utility, especially if the author being studied has a common name as it is possible that papers from different authors with similar names are reported together. Nonetheless, it is a useful site for providing an indication of the number of times a scholar's work has been cited and what their H-Index might be.

Other information on citations may be obtained from Google Scholar

https://scholar.google.co.uk/

Cite this for me

http://www.citethisforme.com/

Excel for statistics

It is seldom realised just how powerful the statistics function is in the spreadsheet package Excel. However this product does have its limitations, some of which can be overcome by using an add-in utility such as Transform Excel, which may be found at:

http://tinyurl.com/gqfmvve

Writing skills and style:

There are numerous utilities which can help research students improve their academic writing skills for example:

Graduate Academic Writing

https://www.youtube.com/watch?v=SNJAMxiOmkU

Critical Thinking and Scholarly Writing Video

https://www.youtube.com/watch?v=oHBtEb_gzjQ

1500 resources to help you write better

http://oedb.org/ilibrarian/150-writing-resources/

Writing and punctuation tips to aid writing up your research

http://www.dailywritingtips.com/

The 5 features of effective writing

http://www.learnnc.org/lp/editions/few/684

Organising books and videos etc

Academic research produces large quantities of data, as well as many books and other academic reference material such as academic journals. It can be a major task to manage all of this material successfully. There are various papers on the web that give advice about this matter, one of which is:

9 Ways to organise Books: Which is your style?

http://www.apartmenttherapy.com/organizing-books-136728

Delicious Library is a media cataloguing application for Mac OS X, developed by Delicious Monster to allow the user to keep track and manage their physical collections of books, movies, CDs, and videos:

https://www.delicious-monster.com/

https://www.youtube.com/watch?v=6CG9BPaSQuM

Buying used books

For the purchase of older books besides the Amazon used section there is also an interesting collection of vendors available at http://www.abebooks.co.uk/

Presentation of content

Wordle.net offers an interesting way of indicating the content of a text file by reporting of the frequency of the words used in the form of the relative size of the words. See the cover of this book as an example of a wordle.net report.

Creating your own personal website

There are a number of applications available with which a website may be built. A list of some of these is available at

http://tinyurl.com/gldj9mn

A popular application for this is

https://wordpress.org/

Building a collaborative knowledge base

A group of researchers may wish to develop a joint knowledge base in order to share their discoveries. This can be achieved by building a private repository of information through the use of a wiki application. A discussion of how to do this is available at

http://tinyurl.com/jhdu345

Creating your own magazine

Flipboard is the leading product in this respect and can be viewed at

https://www.youtube.com/watch?v=97dU6Gzc3JA

https://www.youtube.com/watch?v=6_zm9a5_Ego

ORCID

Open Researcher and Contributor ID (ORCID) distinguishes each individual as an unique researcher. There can be no confusion with the same or similar names.

http://orcid.org/

UK Data Service

A repository of quantitative and qualitative data on a wide range of subjects.

http://tinyurl.com/go637ob

RSS Feeds

 An RSS feed (Rich Site Summary or often called Really Simple Syndication), is a platform to gain a summary of updates from a website in a concise manner. It uses a series of web feed formats to produce a summary of frequently updated information, e.g. blog entries or news headlines.

http://www.whatisrss.com/

Users can subscribe to feeds by either entering the URL of a feed into the reader software or by clicking the feed icon in a browser. The RSS reader checks the feeds which the user has subscribed to regularly for new information and can be set to automatically update and download anything new.

RSS systems most commonly used by websites can be identified by an orange and white button which allows users to add the content of the website to their feed.

http://www.feedicons.com/

Whilst most RSS feeds need to be used in conjunction with reader software many readers will also externally email the content to a users own email address.

Some points of more general interest including dissemination

It is a mistake to try to be too prescriptive about the ways in which the Internet and the Web impacts academic research. What has been described above are the most obvious applications researchers can use in order to facilitate research. But of course there are many others, and these vary according to the topic being researched, as well as the faculty in which the research is being conducted and also in accordance with each researcher's own particular skill set and outlook.

There are many other teaching and learning websites which may be of interest to the scholar.

Making Better PowerPoint Presentations

http://tinyurl.com/hjpa8q2

How to facilitate learning

http://tinyurl.com/jzxqjub

To build a successful academic career, you need to play by the rules

http://tinyurl.com/je3njfu

How to get published in an academic journal: top tips from editors

http://tinyurl.com/z2vttqk

Digital Disruption: Education

https://www.youtube.com/watch?v=daDYlgYxfzA

5 Tips for Publishing Your First Academic Article

http://tinyurl.com/zg3jq9w

Trust and Privacy Concern Within Social Networking Sites: A Comparison of Facebook and MySpace

http://tinyurl.com/hgsy94g

Change Blindness – when small changes go unnoticed:

https://www.youtube.com/watch?v=uO8wpm9HSB0

Bryan Alexander - Digital Storytelling (1 hour lecture from Case Western Reverse University)

https://www.youtube.com/watch?v=tq-4hJEihWE

20. Will the Web and the Internet change the essential nature of scholarship?

Although the Internet and the Web have had a major impact on the practice of scholarship to the extent that many novice researchers have been heard to say, "How could anyone do research in the old days without any of his or her favourite applications available to them?" It is important to point out that these new facilities do not change the essential nature of scholarship.

Scholarship is about the researcher developing him or herself into a leading authority in his or her chosen topic by the creation of new knowledge. This means that the researcher has to become fully familiar with all the important previous research. He or she has to be able to use this knowledge to be able to craft arguments about what is actually known and what needs to be discovered. The researcher then has to make his or her own contribution to the body of knowledge.

At the heart of scholarship is knowledge and rigorous argument. These skills can be facilitated by technology but can never in any way be replaced by it.

Therefore, neither the Internet nor the Web will change the nature of scholarship, but rather at best only facilitate researchers to become better scholars. Unfortunately, as mentioned earlier the Internet and the Web has also increased the opportunities for cheating, which is a significant worry to the academic community.

As previously mentioned there is one other point to be remembered which is that over the last couple of decades there has been an increase in emphasis on the need for academic research to deliver both theoretical knowledge and suggestions of ways and means of putting such knowledge into practical use. This is a new development and it is at least to some extent the result of the openness which is now more common among academic researchers. Whether this openness is a result of the increased level of networking or whether it is a facilitator of this trend to network is hard to say but it is a change in the mind set of academe. Of course, it in no way suggests any reduction in the high standards of rigor required for academic research.

21. Current Action and the Future of Digital Scholarship

To take advantage of the technology available at present it is suggested that academic researchers begin working with at least the five following applications.

1. Create a personal Website in which there is a statement of research interests, what you have achieved so far and some curriculum vitae details and keep this updated as the research progresses. The objective of this is to establish your credentials in the academic community.
2. Establish a Facebook and a LInkedin page and develop a list of contacts. This can be a painfully slow business and thus it needs to be worked on constantly. Your network of individuals who could be helpful to you can only be built by you.
3. Use Twitter to find out if there is a group of people also interested and communicating with one another about your topic or some other topic close to yours. It is always easier to piggy-back on an established group. But get your network going.
4. Start a blog. Find some aspect of your research interest and invite your associates, students and anyone else who you think might wish to contribute. Do not be surprised when this starts slowly but perseverance will normally pay off.

5. Create a database of information, both text and video, references about your topic. This will be in some sense a guide to or maybe a catalogue of your scholarly capital.

As previously mentioned scholarship has changed significantly over the past few decades and the Internet and the Web have played an important role in this. One way of understanding these changes is to reflect on how intensely elitist scholarship used to be. Today scholarship is now relatively speaking much more open and many more individuals are attending university and engaging in academic research activities.

The large increase in numbers of students has been made possible by the connectivity delivered through the technology. This has been the case even in traditional universities which have not relied directly on e-Learning technology. These institutions have incorporated some elements of the technology in their teaching and learning programmes and as a result, the term Blended Learning has come into use. It is likely that Blended Learning will increase in use to support most scholarly activities. In this respect MOOCs have become significant as students are now able to watch some of the best lecturers in the world in front of their classes.

The networking between students and scholars is likely to increase. There is much more sharing of ideas and information than ever before, and this has not only improved the level of scholarship, but has actually made the teaching and learning process more interesting. It is also noticeable how many universities have now engaged in student exchanges with other universities and some of them have even launched jointly awarded degrees. This is likely to become even more significant as language translation facilities improve through the Internet and the Web.

The medium to long term effect of this increased networking could be to reduce the importance of the traditional lecture as a means of dispensing knowledge as students and scholars will increasingly rely on self-discovery through contact with their peers and others. In turn this will lead to more specifically action orientated learning.

The increase in communications facilitated by the technology has to some extent made universities aware of the need to be concerned about the level of service they offer their students and scholars and this is reflected in the fact that some universities now advertise the level of student satisfaction on their campus. It is likely that universities will continue to integrate Internet and Web technology into their processes in order to make their delivery more efficient and effective and acceptable to their students and scholars.

With regard to future developments in technology that can have an impact on academic research it is not possible to accurately predict how the Web and the Internet will develop in the future. However it is most likely that it will grow in reach and scope and in speed and that there will be an increasing number of useful applications for scholars. There are still issues in many locations about the speed of broadband and there are of course still many areas in which there is no signal available. It is likely that there will be improvements in this respect. Also it is probable that the price of the technology will at least in the medium term decline.

This is likely to facilitate even more aspects of academic research, but it is unlikely that it will change the nature of scholarship itself. It is hoped that scholarship will always reflect the intellectual achievements of the scholar in arriving at a deeper understanding of his/her topic and his/her ability to make a contribution to the body of knowledge on the subject matter.

The enhancements we are likely to see to the technology and the benefits available there from simply means that those who are not Internet and Web savvy will be at an increasingly competitive disadvantage to those who are. Of course, as the technology insinuates itself further and further into everyday life fewer individuals will live without a high degree of familiarity with it. But there is a difference between a general knowledge of what can be obtained from the Web and the Internet and how it can be used to facilitate academic research. Thus as the Web and the Internet will continually change this means that scholars are going to have to put time aside to keep up-to-date with these developments, otherwise they will be left behind.

Reference list

Anderen D, Digital Scholarship Tenure, Promotion and the Review Process, (2015), Routledge, London

Borgman C, (2007), Scholarship in the Digital Age, MIT Press, Cambridge

Driscoll, M and E Pierzzo, Ed, (2009), Digital Scholarship Editing – Theory and Practice, Open Book Publishers, Cambridge, UK

Gold, M K, (2012), Debates in the Dogital Humanities, Minnessota University Press, Minniapolis

http://www.aaai.org/ocs/index.php/ICWSM/ICWSM11/paper/view File/2880/3264.

https://www.questionpro.com/blog/how-to-use-linkedin-for-research/

Meloni, J, (2006), Blogging in a snap, Sams Teach Yourself, Indianapolis

Paul M and M Dredze, (2016), You Are What You Tweet: Analyzing Twitter for Public Health, Accessed September

Remenyi D, N Swan, B Van Der Assem, Ethics Protocols and Ethics Committees, (2011), Academic Publishing, Reading, UK, orcid.org/0000-0002-0769-3212

Taylor I, (2016), How to Use LinkedIn as a Research Engine Accessed September

Veletsianos G and R Kimmons, Networked Participatory Scholarship: Emergent techno-cultural pressures toward open and digital scholarship in online networks, Computers and Education, Vol 58, Issue 2, Feb, P 766-774

Appendix 1: A Note for Establishing a Facebook Group

1. Set up a Facebook account and under the heading create (on the left sidebar) select the option group
2. Name your group and add some people to your group. People can be added using their email addresses
3. Select the privacy settings for your group: Public group, closed group, secret group
4. Press create to establish your group
5. Enter a statement concerning the topic for which you would like to engage your group in discussion
6. Expand the number of people in your group by either adding members who are already on Facebook, or distributing the link to your page
7. Individuals may be able to view your Facebook group without having to have a Facebook account but they will not be able to actively participate. For full participation encourage individuals to sign up to Facebook.
8. This is somewhat dependent on your security settings but, only public groups can be viewed freely by non-Facebook users. Closed and Secret groups will require the individual to 'join' the group which requires them to have a Facebook account
9. You can upload photos, videos, or any other digital materials which you wish to share with your group
10. Check your Facebook group regularly and keep yourself to the discussion and invite others to join
11. If you wish, you can delete the group by removing all its members and then yourself.

Appendix 2: A Note on using Twitter to explore research connections

1. Open a Twitter account
2. The first place to start is the twitter search bar. It is often effective to search your topic of interest as a hashtag (#) to see who's talking about it and what they are saying. Hashtags are words with the character # in front of them – hashtags are always without spaces between the words i.e. #SocialMediaResearch
3. The first level of results will provide you with a list of everyone who has tweeted in the public domain using that hashtag. The tweets can be varied, containing images, videos or links. These can be interesting to browse to understand the discussion in the field you are interested in. This can also be used as a tool to find individuals who are interested in or perhaps specialise in your topic
4. It may be of further interest to explore the profiles of those who are tweeting content which you find interesting. They may be tweeting more content which is related to your field, but if it does not have the hashtag you have searched it will not appear in your preliminary search
5. If a user's profile is public you can directly tweet them and potentially establish direct contact
1. Using #SocialMediaResearch on Friday 28th October 2016 there was an endless list of individuals who had tweeted using this hastag and the researcher needed to have the skill in being able to identify those tweets which constitute a source of useful information to his research activities. This is not trivial and requires some considerable experience and it can be quite time consuming.

Appendix 3: A Note on the Facebook Group associated with the Seminar

Alongside this User's Guide, a Facebook group has been established for the attendees of the Social Media and Digital Scholarship Seminar held at Cedars Conference Center, University of Reading, November 16, 2016.

This group has been created as a support device to be used along side this Guide to explore the issues and applications being used in this field.

The group title is "Social Media & Digital Scholarship" and can be found at the following link:

https://www.facebook.com/groups/680234778819832/

Over 150 links which are referenced in this book have been shared in the Facebook group for the reader's easy viewing.

Furthermore the Facebook group welcomes you to utilise the group as a platform to contribute, discuss and share ideas around this topic, and to network with fellow scholars.

This group has been established using the same methods disscussed in Appendix 1, "A Note for Establishing a Facebook Group", and has been set to a closed group. Therefore only individuals who are invited to the group/attend the seminar will be able to see its content.

Appendix 4: A note on how to start a research blog and profile on Wordpress

1. Get started on the Wordpress.com website – if you are new to it, sort out a username etc. This gives you access to all editing tools, quick start blogs and searching for other blogs that interest you.
2. Choose a general field e.g. education and then choose a rough idea of the layout you like – try to include some images, it makes the blog more attractive to readers
3. You are then offered a choice of themes. You can always change them later. Try out a few, when you have decided what you want to appear on your landing page. The more you can keep your landing page updated, the more traffic it will drive to your site. Static blogs are a contradiction in terms!
4. The blog on the front page is for your regular contributions – consider adding reviews of what you have read and conferences attended, talk about issues in your research, link to other sites, images, publications and people to drive traffic to the blog.
5. Using Wordpress, in addition to the blog, you can set up any number of separate pages – consider using one for your up to date publications list (use a standard format so you can always paste this directly to your CV as needed), perhaps another page to store comments, ideas on a particular research theme, links to particularly useful research sites, journals you use a lot, portals and databases.
6. If you use Twitter, consider linking it to your blog – you can display your Twitter stream on the blog to keep more active content appearing. (But don't do this if many of your tweets are not research-related!)

Appendix 5:   A Note on Edublog

Edublog is a blogging service, powered by WordPress, which is aimed specifically at educators and students. Edublogs suggest their service can be used for a range of functions, including sharing materials including videos, podcasts and other media, facilitating online discussions and collaboration, sharing lesson plans, and receiving feedback. Whilst most of this is common to any blogging site it is unique in its facility to create a 'class blog', which can allow only invited pupils to view, share and discuss posts.

An account can be set up easily using an existing email address at http://edublogs.org/

Appendix 6:   A Note on Researchgate

1. Sign up on Researchgate.net website
2. Choose your category e.g. academic, and give your, name, institution and institutional email
3. A few more details and your account request will be checked – fast if you subscribe from a recognized research institution, manually if you have no institutional affiliation. Once you are recognized you receive an email to activate the account.
4. Researchgate allows you to find colleagues and their research, and to answer questions in relation to your field, and ask others to help you. The more questions you answer, the more active you are considered to be.
5. If you have publications trackable online, Researchgate will find them and check with you before adding them to your profile. You can also add publications manually. The best way is to upload a full text version, but do check if your publisher allows this.
6. You will occasionally get full text requests from other researchers – good to respond if you can, and if you cannot upload a full text document to the site, you can send one by private message to those requesting it.

Appendix 7: A Note on Eduroam

Eduroam https://www.eduroam.org/ offers a service targeted at students and researchers within universities which allows its users to obtain internet connection at any participating institution, allowing individuals automatic internet connection using their established username and password provided by their home institution. Eduroam has a global reach and once a student or researcher is established with an account the use of this service is routine.

Eduroam has established itself as a primary internet service across the UK, and has a presence in over 70 countries around the world. You only need to set up your device once at your home institution, and then you can log in automatically wherever the Eduroam network is available.

There is a comprehensive description of the service on the Website.

An account of the development of ICT in the academic process through the experiences of one scholar

This account documents the development of digital scholarship from the 1970s, a decade which saw the invention of email (1971) and the Post-It note (1974). Using personal experience of academic research in four phases (undergraduate, postgraduate and doctoral study, concluding with research activity in the current decade), the account demonstrates the technologies used and the affordances, benefits and disadvantages experienced.

Phase 1

Sue Greener undertook a first degree from 1970-1974 through full time study at the University of Sheffield, UK. Subject disciplines were Philosophy, French and Economics. Study was completely bounded by a) immaturity in relation to research development and b) the gate-keeping power of the academic staff.

What technology was available at the time?

- Books from the university library with significant limitation on number and duration of loan. Borrowing a book involved a search of the shelves or the library catalogue which was a card index in stacked drawers, a paper form for manual completion, handed in after queuing at the desk, manual completion of borrowing and return dates in the attached slip in the front of each book. Popular books for study were generally out on loan and might never return. The main option was to buy books.
- Nationwide electricity shortages meant torchlight for some library searches, and certain examinations sat by candlelight in

1973. This of course was a temporary problem due to the miners strike.

- Business newspapers were available on microfiche – sheets of film containing many small photographs of newspaper pages which could be moved through in counter-intuitive movements on a large desk-based machine which magnified the pictures for reading.
- Although the floppy disk was invented in late 1970, computers were owned by institutions, taking up considerable space as mainframes, and linked to terminals similar to teleprinters. During my undergraduate studies I was required to learn BASIC (Beginners' All-purpose Symbolic Instruction Code) which had been invented by Kurtz and Kemeny in 1964, but this was actually used only in Computer Studies at the time where BASIC and Fortran programming languages were taught. Many students found these inaccessible.
- Information was presented by lecture and seminar, very occasionally supported by a paper handout of notes. Study notes were all on paper in piles of files. Presentations, where there were any, were given on overhead transparency slides using an overhead projector. OHPs had become widespread in the 70s in classrooms and lecture halls (originally invented in the 1870s). Chalkboards still commonly used.
- Language studies required various dictionaries which sometimes had to be brought back from the country of origin if acronyms or current usage was required. Ordering books was done through bookshops and took a considerable time. Repetition and drilling was considered vital in language learning, used in "high tech" language labs where each student sat with headphones and minimal controls, while control was with the tutor at the front of the room, able to listen in to everyone's feeble attempts.
- Various books were required for seminars so bags were a big feature of daily life. Other than a student subscription to the Financial Times there was little access to economic news. The

lecturers were gatekeepers to knowledge, dictating what must be read and offering few if any alternatives.

- Timetables were published and changed on notice boards, as were degree results.
- Phoning home was at public phone kiosks from the street or student residence.
- Sadly programmable calculators were not available until after I left university (1978) but there was plenty of vinyl and cassette players for musical downtime.

Phase 2

Sue Greener undertook part time Masters study for an MBA at Aston University in Birmingham 1980-1983.

What technology was available at the time?

- Study materials were still transmitted by lecture and seminar but at this stage, handouts were much more common. These were often reproductions of overhead transparencies (PowerPoint did not appear until 1987).
- Many lecturers would handwrite on OHP film which was rolled over the projector. Legibility was often compromised.
- Sinclair ZX spectrum was launched in 1982, although it didn't reach many students until later, and then proved of limited use, running a version of BASIC.
- While all note-taking and assessments were done by hand on paper during the degree the final dissertation employed a correcting typewriter using carbon paper for copies. The correcting typewriter showed a small LCD display of the last few words typed, allowing corrections to be made without the need for correction fluid. The electronic typewriter used a daisywheel, as these were faster than the former "golfball" heads for typing.
- However databases were yet to arrive so it was manual card indexes for reference and note retrieval. Interview data was recorded on cassette tapes and played back for manual typing of transcripts.

- Despite this being postgraduate study, at no time was it considered appropriate to make contact with other academics except for tutors and dissertation supervisor. Finding their phone numbers would have been tricky.
- Video cameras and VCR cassette tapes and players were popular from the 1980s, becoming useful for developing presentation skills training. Being videoed was a strange and frightening thing in the 80s for students and delegates. Cameras used the compact cassettes which required a transfer cassette of bigger proportions to play in the VCR.
- After graduation with the MBA, technology began to develop fast using the Amstrad PCW8512 word processor with 512Kb RAM using Locoscript software. From there WordPerfect and finally Microsoft Word became a de facto standard for for text production. No more manual correction. No more carbons. Online dictionaries – a whole new world.

Phase 3

Sue Greener started doctoral study part time in 2001, achieving an Education Doctorate (EdD) in 2008.

What technology was available at the time?

- As doctoral research began and ended with a relevant grasp of literature, search, retrieval and storage of information about literature became critical just as technology began to provide great solutions. Research focused on the development of virtual learning environments and blended learning at a time of transition into these concepts which were new at the time.
- The World Wide Web available from 1991 – a treasure trove for academics.
- Microsoft PowerPoint had become the presentation tool of choice, although Prezi was quickly adopted by some for more interesting approaches.
- Although a locally developed virtual environment was initially used for the research, this was quickly replaced by a standard Blackboard VLE across the university. Studying its effects on

learning and impacts on students so as a teacher became engaged in the development on new materials for learning. CD-Roms had already come and pretty much gone, although they were still helpful to give away as repositories of information, something now undertaken on tablets for many students.

- The university library was now equipped with fully computerized search and order facilities, and offered access to databases of literature. Endnote was the preferred software for storing references and notes on reading, although it was still usual to print out much of the relevant literature found and decorating the house with piles of it.

- A serious change had occurred in terms of access and communication: it was possible and relatively easy to search widely for relevant literature, and to contact a wide range of experts by email.

- Interviews with academics were set up by email, and still recorded by cassette recorder but these were much smaller and digital in nature, compared to those for postgraduate interviewing.

- Journal websites now provided wide searching possibilities and Wikipedia was launched in 2001 – although there was much disinformation concerning its use.

- Although NVivo software was available and taught, many found it easier to stick to manual methods of conducting grounded analysis of transcripts, using highlighter pens, and a coding system developed in Microsoft Excel. However the complexity of the coding system and analysis led some individuals to build their own Microsoft Access database to store and categorise all codes, references and interview/respondent detail.

- Producing the text was done in Microsoft Word using a master document to control sections and pagination. Preparation for supervision meetings involved printing out much material as they preferred it that way, even if email was the principal form of academic communication.

- There was no "cloud" so backup schedules were really important: all data was held and stored on desktops and laptops both of which were vulnerable to crash or loss. Beginning with disk backups, some individuals moved to hard drive backups as small portable hard drives became available.
- Although the Virtual Learning Environment was growing in usefulness and ease of use for undergraduates, the offer for research students was minimal, with a much greater emphasis on tacit knowledge passed down by supervisors.

Phase 4

Sue Greener as post-doctoral researcher today – what technology is now available?

- To what extent has it been maturing cognitive ability and researcher development which has opened my eyes to the vast networks of knowledge available? It cannot be only the technology, yet it is thanks to digital scholarship tools that I can work now at much greater speed to access new and changing information through social media and the World Wide Web. There is plenty of rubbish along with the nuggets, but that is down to skills of judgement and evaluation – these things have not changed.
- From thesis onwards there have been many conference presentations, publications of chapters, books, articles and the opportunity to continue to learn by editing an academic journal. None of these activities happen without technology. Facebook was developed in 2004, hitting 100 million users by 2008. I had joined in 2007 and both this and my Twitter stream are full of conference pictures and comments.
- Now I use Twitter to connect with experts in my research field, following their blogs and writing my own, I run social media showcases and connect with students and staff on LinkedIn.
- Every meeting I attend has an entry in Evernote, which, being fully searchable, means I can always find those little ideas and notes from every encounter.

- Sharepoint and iCloud have solved my data backup issues.
- Aspire has replaced Endnote for me through my institution has a key repository of references for research and teaching, as well as digital reading lists for students.
- I run an online undergraduate course using video casts and live chat.
- I mark and review and moderate assessments and journal articles fully online via cloud software, submitting and editing through Manuscript central/ScholarOne.
- Most of my news is consumed through an aggregator called Flipboard, where I also publish magazines for different groups of students to follow.
- My YouTube channel carries simple video casts as well as privately sheltered student and staff presentations.
- Student and staff encounters are more likely to be fixed by text than email. Although email alerts such as Calls for Papers, and updates from blogs I follow still form part of the daily workload. Meetings are regularly held through web conferencing software.
- My institution's online library search and retrieval facilities have improved hugely in efficiency, together with ResearchGate and Scholar Google. Subscription to Box of Broadcasts allows us to bring professionally produced documentary and other programming into learning and teaching.
- The grip of the Virtual Learning Environment has been loosened and we are able to use a broader range of tools – Edublogs, Mahara for eportfolios and a range of sites for connecting with people and manipulating material – videos, infographics, images.

While this account documents a rapidly developing timeline of digital technology and its application to research, the challenges which such technology continues to offer researchers, both cognitive and mediative, involving precious time to learn and update and apply, remain considerable. There is no doubt we can do more and faster. There is no doubt we can connect with more work, more literature, more fields of expertise. There is also no doubt that the potential for superficial learning through a bite-size cut and paste culture has grown too. Authentic research is not made easier by digital technology, but its capability, its reach and its network has moved from the confines of the individual institution to the world.

Sue Greener

November 2016

Index

academic career, 82
academic research, iii, iv, v, vi, vii, x, 1, 2, 6, 9, 15, 17, 18, 20, 22, 23, 25, 26, 27, 28, 82, 86, 87, 88, 89, 90, 99
academicearth, 29, 30
alcs, 71
analytical capability, 58
blog, ii, 45, 47, 48, 54, 81, 87, 91, 95, 96
brochureware, 5
caveat emptor, 22
cloud, 20, 26, 64, 73, 74, 75, 104, 105
cloud-based system, 20
data mining, 10
dialogue, v, 30, 41, 50
digital libraries, 71
digital literacy, 6, 13, 15, 25
digital scholarship, i, iii, vi, viii, ix, 13, 14, 39, 91, 99, 104
discussion, iv, 1, 5, 47, 48, 50, 80, 92, 93
dissemination, 58, 69, 70, 82
dissertation, iii, 18, 35, 101, 102
e-Learning, 37, 88
embarrassment, 20
embezzle, 21
empirical research, iv, 40
e-Research, iv
etiquette, 50
experiments, 57
facebook, 2, vii, 49, 94

face-to-face, 19, 57
focus groups, 57
followers, 51
fraudsters, 21
funnel, 2, 17
future, 1, 20, 74, 89
google, 27, 28, 58, 77
hangouts, 58
hashtags, 49, 52, 93
help, 17, 23, 31, 45, 77, 78, 97
institutional repositories, 70
intellectual property rights, 35
interpreting the findings, 67
linkedin, 54, 91
macro-processes, 67
mixed methods, 40
mooc, 30
networking, 30, 71, 72, 86, 88, 89
Non-Web, i, 9
on-line, 25, 67
open access, 29, 70
primary data, 57
privacy, 51, 92
qualitative data, i, 10, 61, 81
quantitative data, 9
questionnaires, 57, 58, 61
repositories, 3, 20, 36, 64, 70, 103
research processes, i, 20, 67
sas, 10
secondary data, 53, 57, 59
security, 74, 92

sine qua non, 23
social media, i, vi, ix, 3, 5, 13,
    14, 31, 39, 48, 50, 51, 53,
    57, 63, 104
social networking, 26, 72
stakeholders, 14, 55
structured literature review,
    44
theoretical research, 41
thesis, 104

timeline, 7, 51, 105
trolling, 54
twitter, 51, 52, 54, 93
two-way communication, 5
video blog, 48
wikipedia, 10, 29, 36, 74, 75
youtube, 7, 11, 14, 33, 40, 41,
    44, 45, 61, 62, 65, 78, 79,
    80, 82, 83